REFLECT & EXPAND

reflect & expand

EMILY BOWMAN

sweet moon press

CONTENTS

This book is dedicated to all the wild and wonderful spirits who have inspired words and wisdom throughout my life.

And a special dedication to Boom, for daily inspiration to create often and openly, bravely and boldly, and for encouragement to bring this book to life...we shine together!

INTRODUCTION

I'm glad you're embarking on this journey, and grateful for the opportunity to sit in the passenger seat and guide you through whatever process feels most right for you.

When this book arrived as a seed in my soul, I wasn't sure what it was going to become. I knew I wanted to share a few of my poems and photos, and the original conception was just a simple book of 12 poems and accompanying photos, one for each month of the year, to be used for reflection throughout the month. Then I had a separate idea to create a reflective growth journal with prompts for journaling, meditation, and/or dialogue. Ultimately, I decided to combine the two ideas into this little experiment.

There is no right way or wrong way to use this book. The poems and photos can be used for entertainment or reflection, or even as little inspiration springboards for your own poems or other creative projects (some of my favorite poems have been birthed from the lines of others' poems or from evocative images!). Feel free to take or leave the reflection/journal/conversation prompts...this is YOUR journey and you get to do it YOUR way. Approach this process with curiosity and just notice what you find yourself leaning toward and what you find yourself resisting. It's all just information you can use to understand yourself better, so please, please, please don't pass any kind of judgment on yourself for what you're doing or not doing.

A few ideas for using this book...

- Since there are 12 poems, it lends itself nicely to the concept of visiting a poem a month over the course of a year, but if the month-by-month format doesn't work for you, please use it in whatever way does! You could do a poem a week, a poem a year, a poem every 6 weeks...do what works for you!

- You could set aside a few minutes on the first day of each month to read the poem and look at the photo, allowing it to just sink in and plant itself in your awareness.
- You could revisit the poem and photo a couple days later, and spend a few minutes in writing/meditation/dialogue exploring what it means to you and what kind of impact, if any, it has had as it has been floating around since the first time you read it.
- If you choose to use the reflection prompts, you can do them all at once or visit them several times throughout the month, week, etc., allowing them to guide you in a journaling session, a meditation, or a conversation.
- If you are using the prompts in a writing practice, you could look back at the end of each time period to see any shifts you might have made throughout that period. It might also be interesting and insightful to look back at previous writings throughout the year(s) to explore and identify ways you might be shifting and expanding.
- If you are someone who bristles at structure and need more spontaneity in your creative/spiritual/growth process, this is not designed in a linear way, so feel free to start with any poem/image that calls to you, or you can even flip open the book to a random page and let it choose your starting point for you.
- You can use the notes/thoughts/ideas page in whatever way works for you. There isn't a lot of room there, so if you're wanting to use the prompts as part of a journaling practice, you may want to use a notebook or journal so you have plenty of space.

I hope this process is meaningful for you and you are able to, at the very least, pause for a few minutes each month to enjoy a poem and an image that might evoke some sort of reflection. At the very most, I hope you are able to use the words and images to explore your inner landscape and expand your understanding of yourself and the ways you interact with the world around you, ultimately leading to growth that helps you walk through your life in a more genuine, intentional, and fulfilling way.

REFLECTION NUMBER ONE

Because Too Late Will Arrive Too Soon

If you need a reason
for love (the noun)
or love (the verb)
consider this:
the companions, the places,
the things, the moments
filling and surrounding your life,
the one you have right now,
have not yet been taken away.
So love while you are still able,
pouring all that you are
into those glass jars of impermanence
teetering on the edge of "not yet"

writing/meditation/conversation prompts

- *what are some of the initial feelings, thoughts, ideas, insights, images, etc. you experienced after reading this poem and looking at the photograph?*

- *what does this poem mean to you? what line resonates most with you?*

- *how do you experience love (the noun) and love (the verb) in your life?*

- *who are the people and animals filling your life currently? what are the places that are important to you right now? what kinds of work and other experiences are part of your life currently?*

- *how are you loving and savoring the elements that make up your present moment?*

- *what would it mean for you to pour all that you are into those "glass jars of impermanence teetering on the edge of 'not yet'"?*

- *reflect on experiences you've had with "too late" arriving "too soon"*

- *is there a practice that would/does help you stay connected to and value your present experience?*

notes/thoughts/ideas

REFLECTION NUMBER TWO

First and Foremost

Find a way to love yourself,
to take your own tenderness
in your arms and squeeze it tightly,
holding dearly every fiber
of your goodness,
embracing all those things
you wish you weren't...
just wrap yourself up
in the fiercest kindness you can find,
giving your vulnerability
the same sweet smile
you'd give to anyone you love,
writing your mistakes
the most sincere love letter
ever written

writing/meditation/conversation prompts

- *what are some of the initial thoughts, feelings, ideas, insights, images, etc. you experienced after reading this poem and looking at the photograph?*

- *what does this poem mean to you? what is a line that speaks loudly to you?*

- *do you show yourself love? if so, how?*

- *how do you show love to others? do you do any of these things for yourself also?*

- *what are the things you find hardest to love about yourself?*

- *what would it look like to embrace "all those things you wish you weren't"?*

- *what would it look like to wrap yourself up in "fierce kindness"? choose one act of kindness you can show yourself this month*

- *write a sincere love letter to your mistakes and missteps*

notes/thoughts/ideas

REFLECTION NUMBER THREE

Rest

that pause
between what you thought
was important
and what's actually important...

that intentional stillness
that suspends striving
and industry
like strips of clouds
that could, and will,
dissolve
at any moment...

that supple silence
that tucks you
into the quiet cradle
of your essence,
where you remember
who you really are

writing/meditation/conversation prompts

• *what are some of the initial feelings, thoughts, ideas, insights, images, etc. you experienced after reading this poem and looking at the photograph?*

• *what does this poem mean to you? which line stands out to you?*

• *reflect on your relationship with rest...do you avoid it or embrace it? is it a regular part of your life or something you do only when you're forced to? what emotions and physical sensations arise as you think about rest? what did you learn about rest from your family when you were growing up?*

• *how do you rest?*

• *what is "actually important" to you?*

• *reflect on the idea that "striving and industry" "could, and will, dissolve at any moment"...what does this mean for you?*

• *think about experiences in which you've felt tucked into "the quiet cradle of your essence"...what were you doing (or not doing)? how can you give yourself more of those experiences?*

• *how could you incorporate more intentional stillness and silence into your life?*

notes/thoughts/ideas

REFLECTION NUMBER FOUR

Spring Equinox

Discover what needs to emerge,
whatever inside you is tender
as a seedling, tight as a bud...
just give it permission to spring
from wherever it's been hiding
all winter, just waiting
to hear you whisper
the potential it holds,
the transformation
it will create, the journey
it is finally ready to make,
from the underworld
into the light, where it will grow
into something bold and certain,
something ready and real,
something beautiful and necessary

writing/meditation/conversation prompts

- *what are some of the initial thoughts, feelings, ideas, insights, images, etc. you experienced after reading this poem and looking at the photograph?*

- *what does this poem mean to you? what is a line or phrase in this poem that speaks to you?*

- *what is the first thing that comes to mind when you think about what within you might need to emerge?*

- *if you are able to identify something that is ready to emerge, what would it look like for you to give it permission and to "whisper the potential it holds"?*

- *what is a transformation that could be created by allowing it to emerge?*

- *when you do allow it to emerge, how will you nurture it so that it grows into something "bold and certain, ready and real, beautiful and necessary"?*

- *what are some of the things that are still "tender as seedlings" and "tight as buds" inside you, not quite ready to emerge?*

notes/thoughts/ideas

REFLECTION NUMBER FIVE

27

Guess Who's Coming to Dinner

Your shadows, those deep, dark places
even the light fears,
those shadows beckon,
begging for your attention.
And eventually you must face them
with the same curiosity
you'd give to a stranger,
the same kindness you'd give
to a misunderstood child,
the same careful respect
you'd give to a hungry animal.
Stay with them, study them,
use your brightest light to illuminate
the needs, the hurt, the fear
clinging to the darkest corners.
Respond to their neediness
with understanding,
to their desperation with love.
And learn, please learn,
that they are less likely to devour you
when they've been invited
to sit at your table.

writing/meditation/conversation prompts

- *what are some of the initial feelings, thoughts, ideas, insights, images, etc. you experienced after reading this poem and looking at the photograph?*

- *what does this poem mean to you? what is a line in this poem that resonates with you?*

- *what is your relationship with your shadows? how has it changed over time?*

- *in what ways do you notice your shadows "beckoning and begging for your attention"? what happens when you try to ignore them?*

- *which of your shadows do you most try to avoid? which ones are easier for you to face?*

- *what are some of the needs, hurts, and fears underlying your shadows?*

- *how could you show your shadows more curiosity and kindness?*

- *what would it look like for you to invite your shadows to "sit at your table"? what feelings arise as you consider this?*

- *write a letter to your shadows, asking them questions and trying to understand them better, then, using your non-dominant hand, write a response letter to yourself from your shadows*

**notes/thoughts/ideas

REFLECTION NUMBER SIX

Permission Granted

You don't have to be typical...
there is so much beauty
in the parts of you that don't
blend in, that don't
conform, that don't comply
with someone else's
rigid rules. Love those parts
with pride, with peace,
and never be afraid
to let your weird, your misfit,
your little-bit-different
step into the light and shine
all over the damn place

writing/meditation/conversation prompts

• *what are some of the initial feelings, thoughts, ideas, insights, images, etc. you experienced after reading this poem and looking at the photograph?*

• *what does this poem mean to you? which line in this poem speaks most loudly to you?*

• *reflect on how it feels to be given permission to not conform...notice any and all responses you have (constriction, expansion, relief, pushback, etc.)*

• *what are the parts of you that don't blend in? in what ways have you suppressed and/or embraced those parts?*

• *what are some of the "someone else's rigid rules" you've tried to comply with at different times in your life?*

• *what are your experiences with feeling weird and different? how have those experiences impacted you?*

• *what would it look like to let "your weird, your misfit, your little-bit-different" shine out into the world? what's a small step you can take this month to move those parts into the light?*

notes/thoughts/ideas

REFLECTION NUMBER SEVEN

Time to Grow

When it has served its purpose
you will know,
and the wild within you
will speak directly
to your strength
and your courage, compelling
you to crack your way out
of the lovely comfort
that's cradled you
as you've formed.
And as you emerge,
overcome fear
with the thrill of possibility,
and stretch fully
into something more free,
something more alive,
something more you

writing/meditation/conversation prompts

- *what are some of the initial thoughts, feelings, ideas, insights, images, etc. you experienced after reading this poem and looking at the photograph?*

- *what does this poem mean to you? what line or phrase stands out to you?*

- *reflect on a time you knew something had served its purpose and you courageously cracked your way out of comfort and familiarity to pursue the unfamiliar and unknown...how did you know it was time to leave? what helped you leave? how did you grow as a result of leaving?*

- *what is something in your life currently that may have served its purpose? what has its purpose been?*

- *in what ways has the "wild within you" spoken to you about cracking your way out of whatever has served its purpose?*

- *what possibility might await you that will allow you to feel more fully alive, more free, and more aligned with who you are?*

- *imagine cracking your way out and moving toward whatever else might be calling you...what emotions and physical sensations arise? breathe into the spaces they arise, and expand them so that you can explore them further*

- *what is one small step you can take toward cracking out of the "lovely comfort that's cradled you"?*

notes/thoughts/ideas

REFLECTION NUMBER EIGHT

45

Sit and Surrender

Invite yourself
to return to your seat
at the table of trust,
where you are reminded
of the grand scheme
and the greater good,
where you can soften
into the mystery
and release
that desperate grip
on the way you think
things ought to go,
things you think
you need to know

writing/meditation/conversation prompts

- *what are some of the initial feelings, thoughts, ideas, insights, images, etc. you experienced after reading this poem and looking at the photograph?*

- *what does this poem mean to you? what is a line that resonates with you?*

- *what does the "table of trust" mean to you?*

- *in what ways do you find yourself gripping desperately to the way you think things ought to go? when do you tend to grip more tightly (certain situations, around certain people, when you're experiencing certain emotions, etc.)?*

- *what are some of the things you think you "ought to know"?*

- *what are some ways you can remind yourself daily to step back and take a big picture view on the things happening in your life?*

- *when in your life have you been able to "soften into the mystery"? how might you create a regular practice that allows you to do this more often?*

notes/thoughts/ideas

REFLECTION NUMBER NINE

Following Orders

In the stillness I felt
what it was to be the sun,
to slip in silence from the sky
and dissolve the day
at just the right time.
And I felt what it was
to be the crow, to have landed
a thousand times, gliding
to perch on a pile of rocks...
the mastery, the ease
of doing,
day in and day out,
what you were born to do,
what the loudest voice inside you
commands you to do...
doing
without questioning,
without overthinking,
without your stubborn will
marching in the street
holding up signs to protest...
doing
to fulfill something
far beyond you,
something that looks
like purpose and tastes
like instinct, but is
so much more

writing/meditation/conversation prompts

- *what are some of the initial thoughts, feelings, ideas, insights, images, etc. you experienced after reading this poem and looking at the photograph?*

- *what does this poem mean to you? what lines and phrases speak most loudly to you?*

- *in what ways do you feel most connected to your instincts? in what ways are you disconnected from them?*

- *what do you believe about the concept of having a purpose or a calling?*

- *what does fulfilling "something far beyond you" mean to you?*

- *what does the "loudest voice inside you" command you to do? in what ways do you follow the command? in what ways do you question, overthink, and protest the command?*

- *imagine what would it be like for you to live more aligned with your purpose and your instincts...what are you already doing, and what changes would you need to make?*

- *what is something you can do regularly to connect with your instincts and/or your purpose?*

notes/thoughts/ideas

REFLECTION NUMBER TEN

Be It

Your life can be a revolution...
you don't need to march with signs
or shout through a megaphone...
just be your own brand of freedom
and speak reasonably
about things that matter...
listen carefully and think
even more carefully...
create often and with urgency,
knowing that art
is louder than dogma,
and you are a soldier
in a rebellion you may not remember
you joined, an uprising
led by your instinct and carried out
by your voice, your hands,
your fierce, free spirit

writing/meditation/conversation prompts

- *what are some of the initial thoughts, feelings, ideas, insights, images, etc. you experienced after reading this poem and looking at the photograph?*

- *what does this poem mean to you? what line speaks most loudly to you?*

- *reflect on your relationship with your inner rebel (we all have one!)...how have you embraced and/or suppressed it? how have you used it to create change for yourself and/or others?*

- *reflect on the ways in which your life is already a revolution...what have you built? who have you inspired? what bold steps have you taken toward change?*

- *what does freedom mean to you? what does your "own brand of freedom" look like?*

- *how and what do you create? how can you create more often and with more urgency?*

- *if you were to speak more about "things that matter," what are those things, and how would your conversations be different?*

- *in what ways are you using your voice, your heart, your mind, and your hands to contribute to the greater good?*

notes/thoughts/ideas

REFLECTION NUMBER ELEVEN

Imperative

Stand often at the edges of comfort
and allow them to keep you sharp,
to remind you there's so much more,
to hold up mirrors that show you
all the unhealed places...
and open yourself
to the someones and somethings
that will push you right over those edges
and send you soaring
into the big, bold beyond
where you have no choice
but to grow, grow, grow

writing/meditation/conversation prompts

- *what are some of the initial feelings, thoughts, ideas, insights, images, etc. you experienced after reading this poem and looking at the photograph?*

- *what does this poem mean to you? what is a line that stands out for you?*

- *what are some of your edges of comfort? do you usually find yourself avoiding them or approaching them?*

- *how are your edges holding up mirrors for you? what unhealed places are you seeing in the mirrors?*

- *who are the someones in your life who encourage you to push past your edges? who are the someones who actually push you past your edges?*

- *reflect upon a time you pushed past an edge and soared into the "big, bold, beyond"...what compelled you to push past? what did you gain from that experience?*

- *what is a small step you can take in the next few weeks to begin approaching and/or pushing past one of your edges? who and/ or what can support you?*

notes/thoughts/ideas

REFLECTION NUMBER TWELVE

Now and Then

Reflect on your growth,
even (especially!) if you feel knotted
and messy, drowning in darkness...
look through the lens of progress
and notice shifts you've made
on the journey from Then until Now,
and then just let yourself imagine
how many more
you will make from Now
until the next Then

writing/meditation/conversation prompts

- *what are some of the initial thoughts, feelings, ideas, memories, images, etc. you experienced after reading this poem and looking at the photograph?*

- *what does this poem mean to you?*

- *reflect on your growth over the past month, the past year, the past 10 years…what are some of the shifts you've made? which shifts are you most proud of? which shifts have most surprised you?*

- *how could you celebrate the shifts you've made?*

- *when was the last time you felt "knotted and messy"? what could help remind you to reflect on your growth the next time you might feel like you are "drowning in darkness"?*

- *how might you incorporate looking "through the lens of progress" into a regular practice? and how will you regularly celebrate your growth?*

- *what are some of the shifts you'd like to make from "Now until the next Then"? spend some time imagining each shift and how it will feel once you have shifted.*

- *what is a small step you can take today to move toward one of your desired shifts?*

notes/thoughts/ideas

ABOUT THE AUTHOR

Emily Bowman has been writing poetry for many years, finding inspira-
tion in just about anything. She lives in Western Colorado, where she is
fortunate to be able to spend time in both the desert and the mountains,
both of which provide her with an endless supply of inspiring images and
experiences. Gardening is also an ongoing source of inspiration for Emily,
as well as one of her favorite ways to observe and appreciate the changing
seasons and the natural order of things. Emily has worked as a therapist for
over 20 years, and she is passionate about guiding people through healing
and growth. Her experiences as a therapist, along with her own growth and
healing, have given her valuable insights and rich poetic material as she
continues to explore the beauty and complexity of being human.